M000076480

THE OCEAN OF NOW

THE OCEAN OF NOW

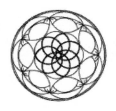

How to Navigate the Unsure Waters of Our

Challenging Times with Courage and Peace

DAVID ELLZEY

Copyright © 2010 David Ellzey. All rights reserved.

ISBN: 978-0615543581

No portion of this book may be reproduced mechanically, electronically, or by any other means, including photocopying, without written permission of the author. It is illegal to copy this book, post it to a website, or distribute it by any other means without permission from the author.

David Ellzey
New York, NY
877-619-1705
david@davidellzey.com
www.davidellzey.com

The purpose of this book is to educate and entertain. The author and/or publisher do not guarantee that anyone following these techniques, suggestions, tips, ideas, or strategies will become successful. The author and/or publisher shall have neither liability nor responsibility to anyone with respect to any loss or damage caused, or alleged to be caused, directly or indirectly, by the information contained in this book.

Cover design and photo: Lisa G. Cameron, ww.cameronartportraits.com
Author Photo: Doug Ellis, www.DougEllisPhotography.com
Editor: Ann Moller, www.divaoftheword.com

Praise for David Ellzey as a Teacher & Entertainer
in the Field of Personal & Global Transformation

*"David Ellzey is an accomplished court jester to humanity.
Through his humor, he connects us to our larger selves."*
Norman Cousins, Bestselling Author
Anatomy of an Illness as Perceived by the Patient

*"David Ellzey is a gifted teacher and healer, and he makes you
laugh! David's new book helps you to joyfully live in the
moment, which is essential for a healthy body, mind, and
spirit."*
Christiane Northrup, M.D., Bestselling Author
Women's Bodies, Women's Wisdom

*"David Ellzey's performance is actually a transformance which
assists in breaking barriers so one may experience the excellence
within. "*
Reverend Michael Beckwith
Featured Teacher in the Film, *The Secret*

"David is a dynamic and gifted teacher."
Sally Jessy Raphael, Author and TV Host

"David Ellzey is a world ambassador of the most important kind. He reminds us to laugh and remember our common humanity. David, I hope you continue to enhance the health of people through laughter and good humor."
Robert Muller, Former Under-Secretary-General of the United Nations

"What gentle power and wisdom lies within these pages, leading the reader simply and beautifully to their unfolding magnificence...Since reading your book, a project that lay dormant within me has come into full form and is already transforming teenager's lives.
Jenny Mullan, Clinical Hypnotherapist, HypnoBirthing practitioner/U.K Trainer, Coach

"David Ellzey is a genius at bringing out the best in all of us."
Helice Bridges, President, Helice Bridges Communications

"I've read and studied with some of the best in the field of personal development and transformation. I can see David evolving to be one of the world's great teachers of the 21st century."
John Aslanian, Consultant and Marketing Director, New York City

Dedication

This book is dedicated to you, the one holding it in your hands in this very moment ~ and to the precious planet upon which we all live. My hope is that this book serves as a map and compass to help you successfully navigate these often challenging times and discover that you can, indeed, have a fulfilling life during your voyage.

Who Is David Ellzey ?
How Can This Book Serve Your Happiness ?

David has had the pleasure of traveling the planet throughout his career, guiding people of all walks and nations to discover the vast potential within - and how this potential can be their guide to a fulfilling life.

Those who have applied the life-changing principles he teaches - and which are included in this book - have moved powerfully through divorce, financial stress, illness, and leadership challenges, and gone on to create more deeply rewarding lives. You will read some of their stories.

David has been onstage before audiences ranging from fifty to five thousand - teaching, entertaining, and inspiring transformation for over a quarter of a million people worldwide. In his private practice he coaches executives, entrepreneurs, parents, and all who desire to master their lives, to live from their true inner voice with courage and peaceful resolve.

David is CEO of David Ellzey Enterprises, and is a co-contributor, with Deepak Chopra and Jack Canfield, to the book, *Stepping Stones to Success*. He is a globally licensed trainer of The Sedona Method® and is a guest faculty member at the renowned Omega Institute.

David shared in receiving the prestigious Raoul Wallenburg Humanitarian Award as a member of the Big Apple Circus Clown Care Program for his work as a clown doctor in the innovative field of humor and healing in hospitals nationwide.

During his successful thirty-year acting career of film, television, theater, and his one-man show focused on humor and personal transformation, he was most honored to have performed at the United Nations Peace Conference honoring Nobel Peace Prize winner Oscar Arias. This conference also had the distinguished presence of The Dalai Lama.

Contents

Acknowledgments

My mother, Jean Glarner Ellzey, for teaching me by showing me what unconditional love really is. My father, Charles Ellzey, for showing me that fun and silliness are essential. My sisters, Christine Ione and Dorie Ellzey Blesoff, for being heartfelt partners in continual self-awakening and learning what the beauty of family really means; My dear friend Helene LaMare, for her unwavering love and support; James Hurley, for being a pure reflection of the playful spirit I never grew beyond; Samuel Avital, who opened the door to my adventure of silence; Hale Dwoskin, for being an inspiration, friend, and colleague in freedom; Lester Levenson for pointing so clearly the way to our unlimited being; Eckart Tolle, for introducing the power of the present moment to so many; Francis Lucille, for his encouragement to laugh and play in life; Ann Moller and Lisa Cameron for their gifts in helping shape this book into its final form. Finally, thanks to the great unseen mystery that is in all things and that is even writing these very words ~ and, more wonderfully, reading them.

Introduction

For billions of years, both massive and subtle change has occurred on this spinning orb that we call home. We happen to be living in a time of both: massive, with many global structures being altered, from economic systems to the global climate; and subtle, with countless human souls experiencing a quiet shift of consciousness from separation and fear to sensing a deeper truth of oneness with all life. Where are *you* in this era of change, and do you feel prepared for these coming days?

The last time you looked in the mirror did you have a feeling of "Wow, what a handsome or beautiful person who is whole and complete"? If you did, I am happy for you, but most likely you had a judgment or two. Perhaps you saw too much weight, too many wrinkles, a person who had failed, or a myriad of other shortcomings.

Most all humans feel they are lacking something important ~ and if they had "it," they'd feel happier, more complete, and finally ready to handle life's challenges. Our poor self-perception is a disease that causes great suffering.

In this book, I will offer cures for this affliction. Using my own personal stories, success stories from my clients and students, and ancient principles, I will guide you back to the sense of what I call "original knowing." This is not to be confused with "knowledge," or things you've learned. All of us have knowledge of many things.

Original knowing is prior to knowledge. It is a boundlessness in which all thoughts rise and fall, and it is unfettered by the appearance and disappearance of life's contents. This knowing has no position or opinion to defend. It is like the ocean which contains all life and yet judges none of it ~ while being an essential part of all of it.

This ocean is what you are: a vastness in which all thoughts come and go. In knowing this truth, one can often find a deep sense of stillness, or a quiet calm that permeates their life.

You have probably experienced being so clear about something in your life and felt its truth so deeply that it couldn't be threatened by anyone or anything.

Similarly, the now doesn't judge the "isness" of its contents. It has a quality of spaciousness in which all the events of life appear and disappear ~ like fish swimming in the ocean but not affecting its infinite nature. My hope is for you to know that the infinite intelligence, peace, and power of this boundless ocean of existence are at the very core of every atom of your being. You are an exquisite and individual expression of this grand mystery and beauty. I will guide you to know how this realization can help you find happiness and success in your daily life.

Throughout the book you will find concrete suggestions for ways to live with more wealth in body, in spirit, and in the world. It may be time in your life for the suggestions or words in one of these chapters to resonate deeply and initiate a more profound understanding of yourself and your existence ~ or you may simply be entertained and moved by the stories. However you experience this book, I suggest you read with an open heart and mind and allow all to happen as it will. And be forewarned ~ the book is spotted with a bit o' humor, just to make it more fun!

From my heart, it's an honor to be with you as you read these words. I do not take this moment lightly. I am committed to the possibility of our time together being life-changing for you, or at least bringing you more peace, if you so desire. Are you ready? Let's jump in ~ the water is warm.

"To know even one life has breathed easier because you have lived. This is to have succeeded."

Bessie Stanley, 1905

Seven Ways to Enrich Your Life, or Dr. Spaghetti on Call

Time to Play

Death and humor are unlikely bedfellows, but on this day, they were an inseparable combination that allowed a final moment to be filled with love ~ and feel like an eternity.

It began with a smear of white greasepaint that I painted on my forehead. As I applied my makeup, I had no idea of what was to come.

In addition to my global travels leading seminars in personal growth, for fourteen years I traveled the corridors of pediatric care units in New

York City hospitals garbed in a white doctor's jacket, clown-suggestive clothing, and sporting a small red nose. As a clown doctor named Dr. Spaghetti in the Big Apple Circus Clown Care Program, I performed humorological surgery, deftly applying a few laughs here and there with children, family, and staff to support healing what could be diagnosed as terminal seriousness, or the natural stress, fear, and grief that arise in hospitals.

On this particular day, my partner and good friend, Kenny Raskin (aka Dr. Mensch), and I prepared our makeup and costumes in the dressing room and then entered the general halls of the hospital on our way up to pediatrics. Chuckles and downright laughter echoed around us as surprised hospital visitors and patients tried to cope with our claims of being the hospital's newest brain surgeons.

We entered the pediatric floor and checked in at the nurses' station for updated information on the current patients. Then we began our controlled and loving mayhem.

We visited a few rooms and were approaching the next when a nurse came running down the hall and tapped me on the shoulder. "Solomon* needs to see you," she said. Kenny and I knew Solomon well. A sixteen-year-old boy, Solomon had cancer. He had been in and out of the hospital for four years receiving chemotherapy and treatment. And he loved us. Normally a teenager might have reservations about being entertained by clowns, but Solomon had an open and loving heart, and a willingness to surrender to laughter and play. We immediately went down the hall to the room, stood at the door, and peered in.

Being Open to What Is

Inside, there was a sense of darkness, of heaviness. We entered slowly, assessing the atmosphere and family. Solomon's parents were Hasidic Jews. His dad was tall with a long, dark beard. He stood on one side of the bed. Next to him

*Solomon is the name I've given this young and special soul to respect his privacy.

Solomon's mother was quietly crying. She wore a traditional scarf wrapped around her head. In the bed lay Solomon, his face pale with pronounced cheekbones. His eyes were open and staring blankly toward the ceiling. His chest was barely rising and falling, with long pauses between. Clearly he didn't have much remaining strength.

We stood at the bottom of the bed as humble visitors, holding a respectful distance, knowing that what was called for here was not our standard comedic fare, but a tender reverence for the reality that was emerging before us, and for the family's clear pain about their pending loss.

Enjoy the Absurd

Finally, with a low and gentle voice, Solomon's father broke the silence. "Dr. Spaghetti, Solomon wants you to sing his song." Kenny and I immediately knew what he was referring to. We now had our assignment. Solomon loved this song for a special reason. It was the classic children's song "I'm a Little Teapot," but with an added twist that.

I learned when I was a kid. The lyrics are: "I'm a little teapot, short and stout. Here is my handle. Here is my spout. When I get all steamed up, hear me shout . . ." And then I add, with a full throaty voice, "Sock it to me, baby, let it all hang out!"

By itself, that might make listeners smile a bit. But what had always added to the impact of this song was something Kenny did that is a rare skill. I began singing the song, while he slowly and ceremoniously removed two small flutes from his pockets and prepared them for playing. He could play them both at once, in harmony. But here's the catch: He played them at the same time ~ but not from his mouth. As I sang the first verse, he prepared his mouth as if he was about to blow the flutes, raised them slowly toward his lips, then bypassed his mouth and did the absurd. He inserted the two flutes straight into his nostrils. After a pause, he started blowing out his nose to play the song in perfect harmony through the two flutes. Solomon had always found this very amusing.

As I sang and Dr. Mensch played that day, Solomon's mother quietly watched Solomon perhaps for the last time, through gentle tears. "I'm a little teapot, short and stout. Here is my handle. Here is my spout. When I get all steamed up, hear me shout, 'Sock it to me, baby, let it all hang out!'"

We were still. The room was still. His mom was still. We all gently observed Solomon. His face remained gaunt and still, not moving. We felt it was time to leave and began to turn when, almost imperceptibly, his presence, as if coming from far away and garnering all the strength he could muster, began to glow from his face. The edges of his mouth began slowly, slowly to rise. Into his eyes a glimmer entered, like an echo of his appreciation. His whole face warmed and smiled gently. To myself, I said, "Yes!," knowing that he had been with us all along.

Have Gratitude for Small Gifts,
Even Ten-Second Ones

The light remained in his face for about ten seconds. Then slowly it disappeared, and his breath stopped briefly. Within a few seconds, his chest rose again and continued its slow pace.

Clearly there was nothing more for us to do. We knew that we had finished our assignment. The father, in his beautiful low and soft voice, said, "Thank you." We quietly left the room.

In our careers in the hospital we see many things. Often we are emotionally affected and need to process the impact of what we witness. Kenny and I continued down the hall, sharing our feelings about what we had just been through. We knew that Solomon was preparing to exit the stage. He was a bright light, a special young soul, one of those who touch you more than you know, until they're gone. Indeed, in our relationship with him, he brought us just as much joy as we brought to him. We were grateful to have had our time on the stage of life with him.

THE OCEAN OF NOW

We walked the halls after visiting his room, and about five minutes later, in a gentle run, Solomon's nurse caught up to us and stood before us teary-eyed.

"Solomon?," I asked.

With a gentle nod, she replied, "Yes."

In such a moment it is always strange, because we search for something else to share, to sum it up, to say about it all. We all loved Solomon. That was enough. With mutual appreciation, she mustered a soft smile, then turned and walked away.

Once more Kenny and I faced the fact that we had the honor of being with patients at meaningful moments at the beginning, throughout, and at the end of their lives. And Solomon's life changed our lives before he left.

We Need Each Other

We so often feel alone in our lives, but it is such a misperception. We share this earth with almost seven billion human souls as well as with animals and nature. Even if our town is a small one or we are in our homes a lot, we still need to interact with others

32

to buy groceries or get gas. We are a social species. Whether we are aware of it or not, we impact who and what we come in contact with. Rarely do we get to see or experience the depth of the impact after our contact. As Dr. Spaghetti, I was reminded over and over that, as with Solomon, the amount of impact each of us has is larger than we can ever know. Keep this in mind, but more importantly, keep this awareness in your heart.

Do What You Love

The impact of our lives is sometimes even deeper when we are doing something that we love that's a joyful expression of who we are. I have led seminars on quieting the mind and living a fulfilled life around the world, and I love leading these events. Yet I was emotionally fed just as much by being a clown doctor. Both are expressions of joy. Somehow, magically, by simply doing what I love, I experienced a young boy named Solomon valuing my presence enough to ask me to help complete his moments on earth before he moved on. Doing what you love and being creative from your heart can surprise you in its impact on others and the world.

Live Fully - It's Never Too Late

Solomon dared to ask for what he truly wanted, even minutes before his last breath. Are you holding back from creating or letting yourself have something that your heart deeply desires? Are you waiting for some past, or non-existent, authority figure to say it's okay?

Right now, can you name something you've wanted to do for a year, or twenty, or your whole life? Our time on this stage is brief. Solomon showed us how to name, claim, and ask for what fills our heart and soul while we still can. He did so even in his last moments. Why wait until then? How else can we fully experience life before our last breath?

A LOVING ACTION FOR YOU

Follow Solomon's example. Choose something that you can do in this moment or sometime today that you have wanted to do and have not yet done. Do it before you fall asleep tonight. It can be to clear away a pile of papers, watch a TV show you've wanted to watch but didn't take the time, get fresh air by taking a walk, tell someone you love them, take a warm bath with candles, or take a break from being responsible to sit in your favorite chair, close your eyes, and allow yourself to simply be.

Above all, do it with the joy of giving yourself the gift. Be spontaneous. Be yourself. Let me be clear. I don't mean spontaneous food indulgence, or reckless use of another substance. If that is your first thought, listen more deeply and see if that inclination is coming from a desire to escape emotions or from an expression of joy and a gift to your heart. Then act accordingly. You know the difference inside. Listen more deeply. Find something that pleases your heart.

That's it.

LET'S CHAT ~ ONE

Your Ecstatic Impulse

What is the impulse that, when listened to, always brings you a sense of happiness? This impulse can help you weather challenging times like these by reminding you to do things that please you, even when you think you *should* be doing something more responsible.

For example, I was recently in a very groggy state in my apartment in Manhattan, having had only three hours of sleep the night before because of  working on a project. In the morning I was thinking I should stay in for the day and rest, but I had the driving impulse to go into the noisy city, of all places. I was moved to attend a class in meditation and yoga at the Chopra Center & Spa at Dream. I followed my impulse, and for the rest of the day I felt wonderful.

I attended a conference once where I heard Deepak Chopra say, "We are microcosms of the infinite intelligence of the universe." He expresses health as "The ecstatic evolutionary impulse of the universe ~ a higher state of consciousness in which you spontaneously make choices that bring joy to you, but also to others in the world." I think he is right. Later in the day, I felt great, and my friends were, I'm sure, joyful that I wasn't as grumpy as I might have been had I not followed that impulse.

So, to follow up on the previous story of Solomon, in case you postponed doing the "For You" action, here's your second chance! Take a moment right now and follow that ecstatic evolutionary impulse which knows exactly what your heart would love for your well-being. Right now, in this very moment, let go of holding back this impulse and spontaneously choose something that expresses your joy. This is a skill. Practice it right now. No joke. This impulse is beating your heart. It must know something. Don't wait for someone else to give you permission. That will probably never come. Go for what you love. It can be as simple as closing your eyes now and resting, with no agenda to achieve and nothing to check off of your to-do list.

If you already did something after being inspired by Solomon, then celebrate the gift you gave yourself and read on. If you are going to do the action now, enjoy! (But hurry back. Einstein and the Holy Grail are waiting for you in the next chapter.)

A Li'l Yiddish Zen Humor

1

Wherever you go, there you are.

Your luggage . . . is another story.

Behind the Stage Curtain
of the Universe
Six Ways to Meet Your Greater Self

Albert Einstein once observed: "A human being is a part of the whole, so called, 'Universe,' a part limited in time and space. He experiences himself, his thoughts and feelings as something separated from the rest ~ a kind of optical delusion of his consciousness. This delusion is a kind of prison for us. Our task must be to free ourselves from this prison by widening our circle of compassion to embrace all living creatures and the whole of nature in its beauty."

The Holy Grail

As a boy, I was on a quest to know the connection of things, what's behind their appearance and to understand how they work ~ including how my own body worked. This played out over the course of my boyhood with me taking toys apart, and my mom giving me an artist's anatomy book to study at age twelve.

Now my Holy Grail involves investigating beneath the surface within myself, my clients, and my seminar participants, to uncover the innate peace, wisdom, and courage inherent in all of us. Time and again I am inspired by watching people's lives benefit from uncovering their greater selves, no matter the challenges of the current times.

A Love Affair with Presence

At age fourteen I got my first glimpse behind the stage curtain of this amazing universe. One summer night during a family vacation I was alone on the endless plains of Texas, where my family has some ranch land. I was standing under a starry sky and was in awe. Stars blanketed the cosmos from horizon to horizon. My feet were on the earth, but I felt as if the rest of me was magically standing in the nighttime heavens.

In one specific moment I suddenly had this sense that the cosmos was actually intimately looking at me. In that moment I knew what being infinite felt like. I had a feeling that the sky was permeated with an invisible and boundless Presence. This Presence would call me forward to seek it for the next fourteen years. It has had many names throughout human history as humankind has awakened to its existence.

That night, and thereafter, I wrote prose and poetry to this Presence as if I were having a love affair with an unseeable, yet ever-present, lover. My writings were always asking for another glimpse or a clue that would help me know this lover more fully.

When I went back to my bed that night, the following words ~ about living as who you truly are ~ came forth. I had realized, in the expansive intimacy of that moment on the plains, that being real or authentic was somehow a key to my having a rewarding relationship with this Presence, to others, and ultimately to life itself:

Life is a puzzle

Each person to his place

But only do you fit

When you show your real face

So don't put a mask in your place in the puzzle

It isn't going to fit at all.

~~~

Right now, can you think of where in your life you are wearing a mask and covering up a more real sense of who you are? Remember Solomon. Do this before your life is at the same point as his was. Are you willing in this moment to pause here, and give yourself the love and permission to be more true to yourself? Take your time here. This moment is not a superficial one. Relax, lower your shoulders, breathe, and consider actually caring for yourself enough to be true to yourself. If this brings calm, feel free to close your eyes and peacefully rest here. If it brings up emotions, be still and welcome them like a loving mother welcoming a crying child. Just be softly present. Remain here and allow the feelings simply to be without an agenda of trying to make them different. Simply "being and allowing" is often enough. If you wish, close your eyes now and take your time.

~~~

Shaping the Formless into Form

My boyhood quest for meeting this Presence soon translated into studying how to see the unseen ~ how to make the invisible visible ~ through the performance art form of mime, also known as pantomime. My mime teacher, Samuel Avital, at his school, Le Centre du Silence, used spiritual principles explaining how the universe is born into form out of formlessness and how the body is one gateway for this manifestation, both in performance and in life. He'd give us the assignment of creating worlds and stories carved in silence on the empty stage for others to "see" without the use of any props except our bodies and space.

In the ancient language of Sanskrit, the word *akasha* means *space* or that out of which all of the universe appears. Onstage, our success in clearly crafting these detailed worlds in empty space was dependent on how unlimited we were in our own thinking and in the use of our bodies. It required us to move beyond old perceptions of who we thought we were and what we thought we were capable of. It invited us to perceive the potential of what was always there, yet previously unseen. Essentially, we were challenged to know that we were more than just a human body with its limitations. Indeed, we were being urged to know that we were the unlimited universe itself. We had to somehow portray the wind, the bird, the tree, the clouds, and the one standing in the forest observing it all.

Similarly, in our lives, like actors onstage, we have access to an infinite potential for something new to be born or created in any given moment. Our ability to manifest our most joyous life depends on our conscious awareness that we are more than just the body and the history of its life. It requires that we be open beyond the limitations of the mind, the known past, and the old roles we used to play.

The Trap Door to the Cosmos

Finally, at age twenty-eight, the quest to know this Presence was fulfilled. I attended a silent retreat led by Michael Bernard Beckwith, who was a friend and an inspiring teacher. During the retreat, something happened. While I was in the middle of a long and deep meditation a trapdoor seemed to drop open within me. What had been a sense of an individual me disappeared down through the trapdoor and dissolved into an infinite cosmos. My body was still perceived there meditating in lotus position and I could hear birds outside, but now my form felt like an empty shell and seemed like a portal to the infinite. Finally, even my body seemed to dissolve into space, although awareness remained.

Earlier, at age fourteen, this boundless Presence had seemed outside of me. At twenty-eight, it was revealed to be my own nature ~ indeed, the nature of all existence. From then on, as I continued to have the normal ups and downs of a young man's life, there was an unshakeable sense that behind it all was something infinite, familiar, and loving. Somehow, now the Presence was not only in the night sky, but permeating my very soul.

~~~

In this moment, it appears you are seeing these words on this page. Clearly, on one level that is what is occurring, but experiment for a moment. What if what was actually seeing through your physical eyes was awareness itself? What if you simply *are* this Presence now ~ rather than the history of your past experiences that you normally define as you? What if, in this moment, there were nothing you had to learn or do in order to be complete ~ no assignment, agenda, or obligation to be productive? Take your time here. Go slow. Pause and breathe. If you experiment with this, you may find that simply being present each moment of your life will give you the answers, actions, and ways to live with more happiness and, needless to say, less stress. Allow yourself to drink from this ~ this nourishing fountain of now.

~~~

The *How To* of Letting Go:
The Sedona Method ®

Soon after the meditation retreat, I learned an eloquent inner technique that accelerated my ability to drop my attention beneath emotions and thoughts to remember this unlimited sense of being when any feeling like fear, anxiety, or grief was arising in me. The technique is called The Sedona Method and was created and inspired by a scientist and engineer, Lester Levenson. After a second heart attack, ulcers, migraines, and more, and being told he had only a few weeks to live, he focused inward for the first time in his life. For three months, in various ways, he let go of and dissolved emotions that had been stored in his body and that had contributed to his illnesses and unhappiness. His body healed and he lived forty-two more years with an unshakeable sense of peace and inner freedom.

Hale Dwoskin carried on the work and is now director of Sedona Training Associates. He has been an inspiration, a colleague, and a great friend. Since I became a global licensed instructor, I now use The Sedona Method as one of my most powerful tools for inner liberation with many of my clients and students.

This technique points to ancient teachings of the unlimited and essential nature of your true self. It is a western way of self-inquiry that helps to drop quickly beneath the surface of a feeling or thought into the stillness and joy of your true self, sometimes in just seconds. It can also be used over time, if necessary, to investigate and unravel old issues to reveal the peace that has always been there. As one of the tools I use, The Sedona Method has supported numerous clients to move courageously through many areas of struggle to create lives filled with more love and success. What follows is an example.

The Hidden Power Within:
A Thirty-Million-Dollar Bankruptcy

One of my coaching clients was dealing with the liquidation of his family's thirty-million-dollar business. His stress and self-judgment were intense. During our sessions, he let go of much of his emotional turmoil and moved through that period with more clarity. He continued to uncover an inner fortitude and calm that has now brought him a new source of income, a great love in his life, more self-knowing, and more overall peace about life itself.

Above all, as we continue to work together and integrate his learning into his daily life, he now sees more clearly when his mind races off to the past or future and steals away his sense of calm in the present moment. The other valuable discovery for him has been finding that being calm is actually more productive than being run by the frenetic energy he had thought was useful, and which had driven his daily life in a number of self-destructive ways for many years. Needless to say, this discovery was life-changing and has brought him greater happiness and health on many levels in both body and spirit.

A Li'l Yiddish Zen Humor

2

Before you criticize your enemy,
walk a mile in their shoes.
That way, when you criticize them,
you're a mile away . . .
and you have their shoes.

You Are Already a Success
Fourteen Billion Years in the Making

If you consider your own life up to now, I imagine you will see that somehow you have made it through some pretty tough times and events ~ perhaps even times you thought you wouldn't escape, and yet, here you are reading these words. There is a life force within you always seeking to persevere and expand. As I mentioned before, Dr Deepak Chopra calls it the "ecstatic evolutionary impulse of the universe."

That impulse is replenishing millions of cells in your body, creating the ebb and flow of the ocean, while simultaneously twirling the planets as you sit here quietly reading these words.

Our task is to remove our inner obstacles to its full expression in all areas of our lives ~ from the body and health to money and relationships.

After fourteen billion years of creating an infinite cosmos, with us as an expression of this creation, it seems clear that this life force is the intelligence stored in every atom and molecule of our being. It guides us in weathering the storms of our personal trials and tribulations, no matter how tumultuous they may seem from our limited perspective. It guides us because it *is* us.

~~~

Let's do a simple exercise to experience a sense of this timeless intelligence.

In a second I will ask you to close your eyes, but before that I'd like you to consider the possibility that your cells are multiplying effortlessly ~ millions in a continuum as you read these words. Your blood is coursing through literally miles of your veins and arteries, miraculously going exactly where it is needed. Just for a moment, consider that this requires no effort on your part. It is the natural impulse of the universe to be alive.

The only thing for you to do in this moment is to lower your shoulders, take a gentle breath (pause and do it now) and simply be aware of this effortless activity happening right where you are. In this moment, you are a localized expression of the infinite universe alive and aware of its own existence. Now close your eyes and rest simply as universal awareness itself. Do this for as long as you wish. I will be here when you return. (Remember, lower those shoulders.)

~~~

This impulse of the life force that permeates all existence is forever revealed and experienced only in this very moment. We live our lives mostly looking in other time zones of the mind, past or future. As a child of the cosmos you are fully equipped to make it through these current global times. We can support this idea either scientifically or spiritually which, in the end, are the same in my eyes.

Scientifically, this spinning orb called Earth, is the result of about 13.7 billion years of life according to the big bang theory. For this planet to even exist and flourish in this seemingly cold universe is miraculous in itself.

The very existence of life on Earth is protected by a thin layer of atmospheric gases. It is a fragile ecosystem. If our human body temperature varies ten degrees up or down, there's a good chance we perish. Yet, so far, this fragile cocoon is magically maintained and we survive as a part of this intricate fabric of life.

We are not separate from this balance of nature. We are an expression of it. According to the ancient health system of Ayurveda, we have within us the five elements of nature and when these are each cared for, we flourish with radiant well being, exactly like a forest and all its contained life does when it's nurtured. Thus, as an expression of nature we have within us this same intelligence that has been creating life for 13.7 billion years. So I say we are pretty fully equipped for handling daily life.

The only distraction from our power and health is the mind's habit of presenting us with data from the past or the imagined future ~ and our habit of believing that the past and future are more real than now. This steals precious time and energy away from living and prospering in the unlimited and fresh potential of each present moment.

The Cosmic Key to Success

The key to success is to live from this cosmic intelligence, rather than from the mind's limited perceptions we picked up along the way from parents, society, or popular culture, and sometimes perpetuated for generations. These limiting thoughts could be: "I'm not good enough, perfect enough, smart enough, pretty enough, thin enough, young enough," to name just a few. All of these are based on the idea that you are supposed to be more than what you are. Where, after 13.7 billion years, could we really be lacking? Certainly not in the ability to adapt or create a rewarding life. We are children of a cosmic life force that has created an unfathomably intricate spinning garden on which we live. We are brilliant flowers of the cosmos, and when we realize that, we blossom.

Spiritually, I look at this intelligence as a magnificent mystery. I am in awe of it and respect it. When I align with it or have quieted to feel its presence within and as me, I prosper. Strangers respond more warmly. I serve my clients with more intuition and wisdom, and somehow I support greater results for them. Projects come to me out of the blue. Plus, I take clearer actions with more confidence, and they have more rewarding outcomes. All of this comes as I dissolve my self-doubt and limiting perceptions of life and radiate confidence and a joy in living.

So whether we support this idea with science or spirituality, we are undeniably a part of a cosmic blossoming in each moment. We can join this unfolding with openness in each moment or we can limit its beauty with rigid perceptions we replay over and over from our past. Whichever we choose impacts our happiness and ensuing achievement, individually and as a planet.

Are We Made of Stardust? Yes, Literally

The atoms that are in the solar system and universe, like carbon, nitrogen, oxygen, and hydrogen, for instance, make up our physical form.

My cousin, Eric Carlson, a successful astronomer, told me that if the universe were a storybook, there would be about fourteen thousand pages, each page with a million words, and our place as humans in our current lifetime would be just a tiny piece of the period at the very end of the book. As miniscule as we seem in this context, we are still a precious part of this ever-unfolding cosmos.

I once heard a quote attributed to the Dalai Lama, that spiritual "practice is for us to ripen our continuum." Notice how this invites us to be present each moment of our lives and yet acknowledge our part in the timeless. Success requires both: being present in this moment and realizing that each single event of life is part of a larger, unseen, unfolding reality.

Often people make the mistake of defining success only in the material realm. Success has two layers, one in the outer world and one in our inner world, and they are related. Having material success, but feeling empty in our soul, is ultimately unfulfilling. Many successful people who have earned millions feel directionless because they have no sense of who they are beyond their material wealth. Having a sense of one's greater self contributes to finding happiness on the way to, during, and after material success. There are various ways to do this, which we will explore in the next chapter.

In the *Real* World
Can One Find Peace During Divorce?

I had a private client who was going through a divorce and felt a great sense of loss because her whole identity was based on her relationship with her husband. He was very controlling and, without being aware of it, she had been willing to be controlled. In fact, that had been her comfort zone until, during our sessions, she began to uncover this transformative insight.

I define success as awakening to one's own power to create life and then doing so. She is now discovering her own voice. She's produced films she had only dreamed of and has begun to explore who she is authentically in all areas of her life. In this discovery and exploration of who she really is, she is already successful in a certain way, and happier as she ventures forth into her life.

Of course, success can also mean financial and material wealth. This can be earning millions or simply having all of your needs and pleasures easily and always met. It can also mean the success of having what is important to you in your life; a life partner, health, being a well-known author, planting a garden you've desired for years, or having whatever brings your heart joy.

So to be clear: The greatest success means having the material things that bring you joy and support your peace of mind in the world while also having an expansive sense of who you are beyond the material realm.

The Collapsing of Time
and Acceleration of the Soul

I believe time is collapsing. What I mean by this is that change is accelerating. Just as in our individual lives, our global ways of looking at things, economically, spiritually, and in the relationships between nations, are becoming outdated. In physics, there is a term, *perturbation*, that might be useful here. Loosely, it refers to how nature evolves by breaking down into what appears to be chaos, when in fact it is restructuring to handle more energy and the next level of its existence.

In the context of what might be called an emerging new phase of earth, our own souls are being called by these times to accelerate their transformation from the past limits of fear-based behavior to a new freedom found in the fresh unfolding of each new moment. We are being asked to awaken from our illusion of separation to a new way of being which is an expression of our innate oneness with all life.

To repeat what Einstein said in the previous chapter: "Our task must be to free ourselves from this prison by widening our circle of compassion to embrace all living creatures and the whole of nature in its beauty."

Stepping Forth in Your Lifetime

For my clients, and for you, this is an invitation to know and live as who you truly are in this lifetime before the final curtain falls. Postponing this awakening actually causes suffering because it is a resistance to the natural urge of the soul's unfolding ~ to grow more fully into being. As I work with clients and students and beckon them to this profound new outlook, it seems to impact them deeply and add greater passion to their lives. It translates as an invitation to step forth from behind the veil of fear and discover the warmth of sunlight awaiting them.

This often means gaining their own voice and hearing infinite life expressing through their own sense of heart. A bright light bulb goes on when they recognize they have the right and freedom during this lifetime to live their own lives, not in reaction to others with fear and anger, but with a proactive sense of self-love. They no longer need to see the world through their past experiences, or through their parents' or anyone else's beliefs. This is extremely liberating for all who walk through this doorway of realization.

Steve Jobs, former CEO of Apple, said, after surviving pancreatic cancer, "Your time is limited. So don't waste it living someone else's life. Have the courage to follow your heart and intuition. They somehow already know what you truly want to become."

Whether you're in your eighties or in your teens; whether interviewing for a job, raising a family, or running a company; if you explore this realization, you may suddenly find more confidence, more peace, and more purpose that is true to your own heart. You can live more powerfully and effectively because your choices are now coming from the quiet and unwavering core of your own true being. This is the "evolutionary ecstatic impulse of the universe" in you bursting forth from the fertile soil of your soul.

The celebration is that one need not wait to know this truth of unlimited being. It is available in this very moment that your eyes are resting on this page. It is your true nature.

~~~

Pause here and reflect inwardly on this possibility that this lifetime is yours, not your parents' or anyone else's. You are a unique expression of existence ~ a cosmic event ~ meant to be fully lived and expressed, free of restriction, and bathed in the realization that you are boundless. You are the localization of the infinite in this very moment of eternity. Take this time. Rest now. It is your moment.

~~~

LET'S CHAT - TWO

My Day with Saint Francis

"Teach peace wherever you go and in whatever you do.
And when necessary . . . use words."

\- Saint Francis of Assisi

In the hillside village of Assisi, as the valley stretched before me across central Italy, my heart calmed and my stress quieted as I imagined Saint Francis standing next to me, atop the very wall upon which I was standing, and saying, "Be still, David, and know peace." As I stood there I gained a sense of this great teacher who once voiced one of my favorite quotes in my life.

Back in time, in a life-defining moment, Saint Francis stood amidst the human carnage and violence on the battlefield and decided to walk away against his family's hopes for him to gain a reputation as a great soldier. After studying to master the art of war, he felt an unwavering voice inside telling him to walk off the battlefield and follow peace.

When the mind is quiet, there is a knowingness that is free of doubt. It is what guided Saint Francis to become a beacon for peace on the planet ~ without hesitation ~ both in his own time and now. He and his life teachings beckon those who are seeking to know this deep and unwavering sense of who they are. He suggested to us that true peace is known beyond words.

~~~

For one moment, come here, behind your mind. Rest in a peace that is not based in doing or saying anything. Allow yourself to simply be.

~~~

Five Keys for Unlocking Success

I want to preface this chapter with the idea that these keys are specific ways of being that, when lived, create more successful results. They are effective because they are aspects of the greater universal intelligence. Thus, when we live in these ways, we are aligning with this intelligence, which has been the creative force of life since before time and is the foundation of our very nature.

Since this intelligence is inherent in all of life, we are resonating with the potential success and harmony latent in all situations. By living in these ways, we help awaken the previously unseen abundance of the universe to come forth into being in all circumstances. In this manner we get to enjoy the resulting riches because we're acting and being in union with that from which all riches come. As Samuel, my mime teacher, said, "We are in league with the formless bringing form into being."

The Joy of Living

The first of these keys is to have a simple sense of joy in living. I realize that in today's current economic times this may seem easier said then done. But it is specifically this lightness of being, or this fresh outlook, that opens the previously unseen doorway out of the current challenges and into other options and potential success.

As I mentioned earlier, since you have 13.7 billion years of creative intelligence behind you and within you, you are equipped more than you can know to make it through tough times. I realize that feeling joy may, at times, feel very challenging. This is why having a personal tool like The Sedona Method for liberating oneself from the weight of emotions is of such value.

The other doorway is to simply see through the veil of suffering to notice that behind it is peace.

Often suffering is tied to what used to be in the past or what we imagine might be in the future. Yet, even the past and future are viewed in the now. In truth, you cannot escape being in the now. Recognizing this can help lighten the load of the pains we recreate and relive from the past ~ and the stressful feelings created by imagining the future.

We know from quantum physics that no event can ever actually repeat itself. So reliving our memories, and using them as if they are real, limits how we perceive the possibilities of this moment. It is like driving a car by watching a past movie of the road placed in the windshield rather than seeing the road itself. In the present moment, anything new and magnificent is possible if you are willing to let go of holding onto the past. It only takes a nanosecond to interrupt the pattern and be fully present.

This nanosecond is the crack in the mind's dam that means your suffering days are numbered and freedom is available, perhaps even as swiftly as now ~ as you read these words. Would you be open to that being true? Pause here and ask yourself, as you sit here reading this book: Would you be open to being free of the past in this very moment? Just plant the seed in the soil of your being and water it with silence. If you wish, take a moment, open inside yourself, and rest now. Let the seed of freedom germinate and blossom into full bloom.

Choose Your Life Team

The second key is to surround yourself with people who support your well-being and success, and whose well-being and success you support. It is important that they care about your happiness and hold you accountable for taking care of yourself and having what you love in life. These relationships are most powerful when they are mutual. This means you both welcome the support that is needed when one of you is down in the dumps or needs to be reminded of the simple magnificence of who you truly are.

Unfortunately, a majority of relationships revolve around focusing on what is wrong in life. There is no shortage of problems to complain about: the economy, health, mortgages, politics, global warming ~ these are just a start. Proactively addressing these issues can be of value, but focusing on them primarily as problems to stew over is an endless circle of emotional suffering with no escape hatch. You can find the path out of this endless circle by devoting yourself to a creative resolution or finding peace, which is accessible regardless of the existence of these issues. Finding partners who seek and celebrate this way of being is a key to living an inspired life.

If you're an entrepreneur or have a business team, then having associates, assistants, or a leadership team that also seek mutual support and positive outcomes is essential. Partners who focus on the positive vision and not the problem are an age-old equation for success in business ~ an equation that has stood the test of time because it is truly powerful. So, surrounding yourself with people that support you living your greatest life, and that you support in return, is an essential step on the road to manifesting your dreams in both business and your personal life.

~~~

Take a moment and think of three people that support your success or well-being, or who have done so over the course of your life. Even if you can't think of three people, celebrate the ones you *can* think of, no matter how many, or how few, there are. You may wish to pause here ~ and simply appreciate the fact that these people have been on the Earth at the same time as you.

If you wish, actually call them and tell them, "I just wanted to say I appreciate you and how you support me in my life. It means a lot to me." Use whatever words feel right for you. We impact others, even by simply calling them to thank them for what they give us. I suggest that if you do call, do so free of expectation or a need for any specific response. Do it freely without expectation of return. Nurture these relationships. They are nourishment for your soul.

~~~

Find Stillness Beyond Thinking

The third key for successful living is an awareness of how quickly thoughts come and go ~ and how we still give them credit as being true. We have the choice to imbue them with authority or not. When we open ourselves to being more than just our mind and thoughts, we uncover a deeper expanse of being, a larger knowingness ~ a greater wisdom about life in any situation, either personal or professional. It is a quiet and unshakeable sense about things. I'm sure you've had moments of this unwavering clarity about something in your life. It comes with a sense of stillness and no need to defend or protect a position.

It is beyond thinking and it is undeniably real. Sometimes it is a quiet knowing that all is well, just as it is. Or it can be a calm clarity about what action to take, or when to take no action, who to call to shift the direction of a company, what people to hire, what friends to have, who to marry, what food best serves your body's well-being. It has a quality of simply being, and yet it can feel very alive. It is like the familiar womb in which we all once existed, except now we *are* that boundless womb of consciousness, giving birth to decisions and our life's activities. Listen quietly. The stillness is always here, just behind thought. Some people call it the heart, the soul, or the spirit. However, even a name cannot touch its expanse.

So, when we listen only to the mind, we hear movie reruns of what *used to* be and what we fear *might* be. As I've discussed throughout this book, focusing on these reruns and fears negates the potential answers and life choices found in the infinite potential of now. The calm and clear knowingness of now is always a more fertile soil for the flowering of answers and the fulfillment of needs.

Taste the Quantum Soup

This fourth key is a favorite of mine. I am not a quantum physicist, but quantum physics has coined a term that I appreciate, which refers to the potential of each unfolding moment. The term is "quantum soup."

Loosely, it means that there is infinite potential in every moment based on the infinite combination of elements that exist. So the contribution of your thoughts and feelings to this moment will be what you're going to taste in this soup. If you view this book as dreaded homework, you will experience it as such. If you quiet the mind and remain open to its benefits, you raise your chances of receiving some benefits.

So what gets in the way of creating success is our contribution of the decaying contents of our past into the soup of the now. This is what covers up the possibility of a fresh and sumptuous new moment.

Watch a child playing and you'll notice they're not usually thinking about yesterday or tomorrow. They're fully and completely in the moment ~ looking at the resources they have and enjoying what's in front of them, whether it be playing hopscotch or building a fort. If we would live more like that, with a sense of moment-to-moment unfolding and using the resources we have to do what's necessary to complete our task, we'd be much more successful. However, as adults we have become accustomed to seeing the present moment through the lens of the past ~ the fort that fell apart last year, if you will, whether that be our marriage, our financial status, or something else. This creates fear and restricts our clarity in seeing the path to a more successful and rewarding outcome.

The past can include both minor and traumatic events and impact the present in numerous ways ~ as in the following story.

Live Beyond War

The fifth key is to transcend the impulse to do battle or create war, both individually and globally. I was invited to contribute to a leadership event at the United Nations by a good friend, Elizabeth Soltis, who was leading this particular workshop. At this nine-day event there were about thirty attendees who were in leadership roles overseeing United Nations development programs in their respective countries. I was brought in to speak of the application of these principles to success in the realm of organizational and global leadership.

One kind gentleman attendee was from an African nation that has a tragic history of tribal war and genocide. As a leader of UN programs there, he had the task, as leaders do, of creating a productive atmosphere in his office and on his team. It just so happened that some of his staff were from the warring tribes and, no doubt, had deep-seated feelings of mistrust and even hatred toward one another. As I worked with him privately, I was inspired by his kindness and willingness to accept the animosity among the staff ~ and yet be unwavering with a quiet knowingness in his vision for harmony in his office. This approach of his portends a greater possibility of success than if he entered the situation armed with his own past fears and hesitations.

I worked with another leader one-on-one. By the end of our conversation, she had moved beyond her doubts about resolving conflict in her office and, for the first time, physically experienced within herself an openness to new possibilities. This produced a big smile on her face. It was a simple, yet meaningful, shift in her perception from a habitual and unconscious way of seeing the world based on her past.

The stories of these leaders are examples of having a greater potential for conflict resolution and moving beyond war: he, because of his resting in a deep knowingness of what was true for his soul and what he was fully committed to without hesitation; and she, because of her new openness to a positive outcome beyond what she'd originally believed was possible.

~~~

The above stories are pretty dramatic and global in scope. But we often feel at war in everyday life, too. This can include being at war with yourself. Is this familiar? A good way to know where you are at war is to ask yourself, "Is there anyone in my life who I wish were different?" I realize this is probably a silly question. It's more like, "Which person on my list should I start with?" This resistance to the way they are is a kind of pushing against, a kind of fighting. It can play out as a subtle or not so subtle battle.

Sometimes these battles can feel pretty deep. I have a question for you: In any of these battles, are you wearing any inner armor to protect yourself or your heart from being hurt? Can you tell how wearing armor requires effort and diligence to defend your beliefs, protect a past hurt, or pursue being right?

If you are holding this book with hopes of knowing a more fulfilling life, then seeing where you have armor up will help. Armor ultimately hinders intimacy and the fulfilling relationships that we all yearn for. Would you be willing to consider letting down your armor, even for this moment ~ here, while you are reading these words? It's safe here. See what it feels like. Take your time. Try it. Take a breath. If you do try it, see if your chest area is a bit more open. Again, take a moment here, pause, and remember: This is *your* life to live ~ nobody else's.

As long as you live in reaction to, or "protecting from," you stay in relationship with that issue, and your life is unconsciously devoted to, and perpetuating, that pain.

I'm going to guess that if you are protecting yourself from anything, it relates to your past on some level. Can you see how in this moment you are free ~ if you let it go? Can you consider this for a moment? Take your time ~ pause here. You ~ and nobody else ~ get to choose when you remove your armor and live more freely.

Today you are learning to take care of yourself. It is your time, your life, your love to have for yourself, your inner strength, your existence. When you are not living in reaction to or protecting yourself from what you *don't* want, you can finally know what you *do* want. Then you can choose more consciously who and what makes up your life. Take a moment here if you like. Lower your shoulders, take a full deep breath, close your eyes if you wish, and rest.

Three Stories of Awakening

From Boy to Man

I often work with men who are searching to uncover their own sense of who they are. This can mean releasing boyhood guilt, shame, or the feeling of needing attention to survive. For many men, liberation means moving beyond their father's beliefs to find their own sense of being on the planet as grown men, ready to have their own fulfilling lives. For others, it means moving out of the debilitating fear of violence instilled in them from a childhood of abuse. For still others, it means letting go of the constant seeking of love in most of their relationships with women ~ driven by a hunger for the love they never received from their mothers. Whenever a man does break through these issues, I am awed and honored to see the shining soul of a man awakened to his own strength, gentleness, and simple being. Instead of the traditional knight in shining armor, I believe we can each become a shining knight with no armor.

One fifty-year-old participant in my men's seminar discovered that the way he actually stood and cocked his head was a result of his fear of always being hit during childhood. Upon realizing this, emotions welled up as he attempted to stand, facing me straight-on, without protecting himself. He recognized this prison he'd been in for so many years. The tears were also in recognition that he didn't have to continue in that fear if he chose not to do so. His stance changed, his jaw squared off. This is an inner journey he has now embarked upon. His task is to practice standing and facing life without hiding his magnificence. In this freedom, he can now discover who he really is. His success will certainly be impacted by this discovery.

From Divorce to Divine

One other category of people I often work with is people who are going through various stages of divorce. If you are going through divorce, this pathway is laden with opportunities to either feel self-pity or to discover that who you are is infinitely more than half of a couple. Success in this context means transitioning from being part of a *we* to feeling you are a whole and complete *me*. Even in partnership you are already whole and complete in your innermost being, but we often cover this up with a false dependence on the partner, as if to complete a seeming lack and incompleteness.

During her divorce, one student of mine found an inner strength and, to her amazement, an inner calm that helped her navigate the tumultuous waters of a difficult divorce. This inner calm led her to see that she had all she needed inside to make it through the challenges of becoming a single mom with a lively teenage daughter. It also uncovered an awareness that she was more than a mother; indeed, she began to feel that she was a woman who felt divine in her own being.

From Pain to Presence

One client I have has been travelling a road of extreme physical and emotional pain for much of her adult life. And yet, amidst her seemingly insurmountable physical discomfort, her laughter and lightness has remained a pillar of her spirit. Needless to say, in our sessions we have found the humor of life, and it has been a welcome balm of relief unto itself. Humor reflects our ability ~ even against the greatest odds ~ to transcend our trials, to be larger than them. It continues to prove that we are more than our circumstances.

As she and I have continued working through both her physical and emotional struggles, it has become clear that, other than laughter, the most effective relief has been bringing her focus of attention from the future, or from reliving her very traumatic past, back into the present moment.

After surgery there has been some abatement of the pain, but her work has continued to be about seeing through the emotional views and perspectives on life that she'd been developing since childhood, and which had been contributing to her physical suffering. With time, there has been more resting in the present moment, and she has often expressed to me that our sessions have been an essential part of her hope in life.

I work with people of all walks of life who are letting go and, in returning their attention to the now, finding peace and the riches of spirit. This is the human journey that we are all on: the journey of awakening to the refreshing renewal available in the now. From this sense of unlimited being in the present moment, creating success and a fulfilling life becomes more of an overflow of our being, rather than a search to fill a painful emptiness. The great news is that a path to success with a sense of overflow requires less effort because our energy and courage are coming from a boundless well within ourselves.

More good news is that, whether growing out of childhood fear, moving through divorce, or dealing with physical pain, the relief is found in the same place: the present moment. As the mind quiets, it reveals the ever-present and nurturing background of the ocean of all being.

LET'S CHAT ~ THREE
Can You Actually Find a "You"?

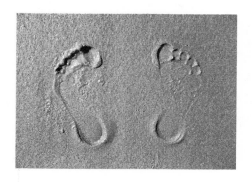

Throughout time, and still to this day, great sages have invited us to investigate and see if our perception that we exist as separate from the universe is actually true. This exploration has the potential of relieving great suffering. Let's go on an adventure.

If you don't go into your memory right now or you don't focus just on your body ~ can you actually find this separate *me* that you refer to in normal conversation? Can you see how it is re-created by the mind each time you refer to it? Can you actually locate it? I know it feels like it is "here," but does "here" mean the body only? Is the body the totality of who you are? Let's explore this further. Certainly there is an awareness of the body, these words, this book, breathing, reading. So we can say there is awareness ~ but can you actually find the defining boundaries of this awareness?

Why are we exploring this in the first place? The egoic sense of a *me* that seems separate from the universe is defined by a past history and endless stories. Identifying ourselves with the past limits the possibility of experiencing a more rewarding life in every unfolding moment. It also creates a false sense of separation from the very universe in which we want to find love, harmony, and success.

If you investigate the seeming existence of an individual *me*, you may discover it is mind or concept-based. You begin to see that you are what can be called awareness itself, or Presence. Feelings, concepts, and thoughts may rise and fall within this awareness, but as you begin to know yourself as this and not the thoughts that come and go, thinking has less negative impact ~ or no impact at all ~ much like clouds in the sky that come and go, yet don't impact the spaciousness of the sky.

Thus, the extraneous noise of the mind is seen through and the most productive thoughts and impulses-to-act can be heard. You can more clearly hear what comes from your deepest Self and what serves your highest quality of life.

This is when lightness and laughter happen more readily. Notice how the mind might say, "Yes, but who is the one laughing or reading these pages?" or, "Sure, but who will pay my rent?" My proposal is that most all of that will go on as usual, simply without the suffering of the ego or "doer" taking either credit for things getting done or blame for things not getting done.

In other words, the infinite cosmos unfolds moment by moment. We have no choice in this. Your task is to do what you love and do what you need to in order to care for your family and the essentials, but open yourself to the possibility that all this can occur without the struggle of the little egoic *me*. Struggle is experienced in thoughts and feelings. You are infinitely more than a neurological thought impulse of the brain or the physiology of an emotion that rises and falls in a nanosecond of eternity. Let go of holding on to this small identity of a *me* and experience a more fulfilling and effortless life.

Let's slow down here and check in. Is the mind quieting or getting noisier at this possibility?

Sometimes the simple recognition that the separate *me* is a figment of the mind or memory has a calming affect. However, if this idea stirs up resistance or a sense of fighting back, then you get to see how real it seems that there is a "someone" who feels they have to defend a position in an attempt to exist. Simply try and actually locate that someone.

Why is this relevant to your life and more than just another spiritual-philosophical conversation? We suffer emotionally and struggle in life because we perceive a *me* with problems. When you investigate and see that this separate *me* is illusory, created by mind and memory, you gain a sense of the unlimited possibilities of life ~ beyond the limiting confines of the behavior and history of that *me*. Then all seeming problems don't actually belong to anyone specific and can dissolve as well.

This quiets the mind and frees you to live with less drama and more love, more courage, and more success. Most importantly, all of this becomes more possible with less suffering. This means less suffering in relationships, about the body or finances, about children or spouses, illness and much more.

Ponder this possibility that emotional suffering need not exist. Think of this like the out-of-state landlord of a run-down building. When you search for the absentee landlord and you find that they never really existed, you are free of paying rent to the problems that have been taking up real estate in your experience of life. You are free.

A Li'l Yiddish Zen Humor

3

If there is no self,
whose arthritis is this?

Where to Now?

For centuries, the spiritual seeker has often entered a period of silence of the mind and then eventually the thought arises, "Okay, what next and where to now?" And for centuries, the answer has remained the same. The answer to "Where to now?" is "Here."

This answer invites you to do one thing: Allow your attention to remain *here*. Thus, no matter what thoughts come and go, *you* remain present. Be more interested in this moment and you can awaken to the undeniable and simple presence of awareness that you are. In this discovery, it becomes clear that there is no place else to go.

In this moment, notice if your mind has an impulse to do more or understand more ~ more than simply rest *here*. If so, just notice the impulse and remain *here*. With time, that impulse loses steam. What remains is a new experience of the spaciousness of now in which all life happens. "Being here" doesn't mean with your body, it means with your attention. You can put your body anywhere. In fact, climb Mt Everest and I recommend your attention stay extremely present, otherwise you can miss a step and lose the very body that you do have.

This will take practice, returning attention to the present at any moment, until there is a sense of never having left. The more this is done, the more obvious it becomes that you are the infinite ocean of Presence and not the contents that come and go. The humorous thing about it is that you can't actually be anywhere else but here and now. The mind can be in other time zones of thought, but you as awareness are only here. Just for fun, without moving the body, go ahead and try to be somewhere else. I'll wait.

Even thoughts of the past and future are all occurring in the now. Thus, as one chooses to meditate or rest in the present, it does not require sitting on a mountaintop or in a comfy chair at home, although both might certainly be nice to do. While being in the now, you can also catch a cab, teach kindergarten, talk to a lover, all while staying present rather than getting on the horse of the next thought and letting your attention be ridden away from the present moment.

It is helpful to move beyond the idea that this is a spiritual concept and therefore not useful in daily life or business. On the contrary: It takes this awakened and expansive state of awareness to be open and see the endless possibilities in a given situation that were previously unseen because of limited thinking.

How to Have Goals in the Now and Manifest Them

There is no contradiction between your heart having a particular joy it wants to experience, and being very present as you work toward the manifestation of this joy. As you move toward your goals, both in life and in business, the first step is to be clear about the heartfelt direction of your goal and yet remain open to the unfolding of the path, even as you are engaged in taking action.

In truth, in considering writing this book, I had no clue how it would look in the end, or exactly how to go about it. Even so, my heart's goal was clear: To inspire those reading it to be open to the greater possibilities of their lives. I mention this because, in this openness, while having a clear intention, and taking action, somehow it all unfolded easily. Pages were filled, I found a team of great people to work with, and a one-hundred-page book was born, which you now hold in your hands.

Now, as a result of this book, my dream has the possibility of manifesting. Each time it's read, the potential exists for a cosmic event to occur. Each soul enters a doorway of words that may or may not transform their existence. My point is, having a heart's intention is essential, but being open to how the path unfolds is equally important. Being open is being free of emotional attachment to the outcome. By emotional attachment I mean the fear and high emotional stakes that cause narrowing of vision and diminishment of creativity.

In the Sanskrit language there is a statement, *Om Anandham Namah.*, which translates to mean, "My actions are blissfully free of attachment to outcome." By being free of emotional attachment you raise the probability of a more harmonious and successful achievement, specifically because you are not pouring doubt and fear onto the path. In short, have a clear heart's intention, take action, then let go and stay open to the cosmic unfolding of your success. Above all, you can then more fully enjoy the journey. The publication of this book could not have occurred as effortlessly as it did without my following the steps I just mentioned.

CHAPTER SEVEN

The Shores of the Ocean

In an infinite ocean there would seem to be no shores. Yet there is a desire in each of us to rest and find peace. We seek a shore to land upon, a harbor from the winds of life, someplace where we can take a break from our lifelong journey, this seemingly endless quest.

I hope that after reading this book you have a new sense that this shore of rest that we seek, individually and as a species, is not found in the external world, but within. Resting happens as we realize that there is no more distance to travel to find this shore. You *are* the shore, here and now, even as your eyes rest upon this page.

As the external world continues its changes and challenges, the more that you rest within, the more calm, courage, and peace you will find during this amazing adventure we are all on together.

Thank you for voyaging forth with me through this book, through your life, and into the present moment. I wish you the greatest happiness as you deepen in knowing your own sense of an unlimited life. It has been my great and heartfelt pleasure to meet you here, in the infinite Ocean of Now.

RESOURCES

1. www.DavidEllzey.com
Events, blogs, audio, and video related to
David's transformational and global work.

2. www.DavidEllzey.com/sedona
For David's Sedona Method event schedule,
blog, audio, and video.

3. www.bigapplecircus.org
The Big Apple Circus Clown Care program was
created by Michael Christiansen and celebrated
its twenty-fifth year in 2011. (212) 268-2500

4. www.Sedona.com
Further information about Hale Dwoskin and
Sedona Training Associates. (888) 282-5656

Coming Soon!

THE OCEAN OF NOW

The Audio Version

Listen to David's calm voice as he shares the powerful principles of this book ~ inspiring you to live your daily life with peace, courage, and a boundless sense of who you truly are.

BONUS: Hear additional thoughts of reflection and inspiration that are not included in the book.

Soon to be available in CD and downloadable MP3.

To book David for keynote speaking, seminars,
coaching, and more:

www.davidellzey.com

david@davidellzey.com

212-996-5159

WHAT YOU CAN EXPECT

Work with David in any capacity ~ as a seminar leader, coach, performer, or via his audio and video products ~ and you will gain powerful ways to:

- Quiet the mind
- Move beyond anxiety, stress, anger, and more
- Take action with calmness and clarity instead of emotionality and reactivity
- Deeply know what peace really means to you
- Gain the gift of laughter
- Step forward from behind the veil of fear
- Communicate with ease and calm self-knowing
- Gain an expansive sense of who you truly are

David at six months... ready to play.

And a 'few' months later . . . playing!

Jump in and join me, won't you?

JOSEPH'S CORNER BOOKS & GIFTS
1515 W OGDEN AVE
LA GRANGE PARK, IL 60526-1721

02/17/17   RECEIPT   03:09:17 PM

347943   NB

Qty. Item/Description   Disc.   Amount

  1 BC-SS17   @ 5.25   T$ 5.25
    SPRINGTIME OF THE SOUL 2017
  1 B-ELL-3581 @ 11.95   T$ 11.95
    OCEAN OF NOW
             MERCHANDISE TOTAL $ 17.20
    TOTAL SALES TAX COLLECTED $ 1.55
                        TOTAL $ 18.75

SIGN X_____
         PATRICIA J GIBBONS

I AGREE TO PAY ABOVE TOTAL AMOUNT
ACCORDING TO CARD ISSUER AGREEMENT

   ACCOUNT: XXXXXXXXXXXX7364
CREDIT CARD: MC - MASTERCARD
    EXPIRES: 04/18
  AUTH CODE: 050914

Thank you for visiting Joseph's
Corner. Please come again.

Retain this receipt for your record.

Clients' Praise for David and His Work

"David is one of those rare master teachers. His teaching was the beacon that guided me to new and fertile territory as I navigated the complexities of a divorce, a growing career, and raising children. I can't imagine getting through it without him. "

- Jan Nolte, Executive Communications Consultant
- www.theinfluentialvoice.com

"Want to talk about someone who rocks the house when it comes to insight, humor, and deep, genuine devotion? David has an amazing capacity to help you focus on what you're seeking, then fully support your journey and arrival. So if you're thinking about makin' some moves, the first move you oughtta make is to contact David, now."

- Pete Grossman, Author-Owner, Infauxtainment.com

"David's a master coach who can dissolve my panic of single motherhood into a place of profound peace within minutes. He effortlessly guides me home to a sense of power where I'm connected and feel held and supported by the Universe. It's as if he lives in another dimension of peace while being in this world, but not of it. David has invited me into a realm of delight, freedom, and abundance. He's helped me be a YES to the mystery of Life. He is rare and precious indeed."

- Allana Pratt, TV/Radio Host, Sensual Empowerment Coach, Author, How to Be & Stay Sexy
www.AllanaPratt.com

THE OCEAN OF NOW

The Ocean of Now
David Ellzey Enterprises
New York, NY
212-996-5159
david@davidellzey.com
www.davidellzey.com